OUR DAILY BREAD
GUIDE TO EVERYDAY LIFE

ANTICIPATING
HEAVEN

MICHAEL E. WITTMER

Our Daily Bread
Publishing™

Requests for permission to quote from this book should be directed to: Permissions Department, Our Daily Bread Publishing, PO Box 3566, Grand Rapids, MI 49501, or contact us by email at permissionsdept@odb.org.

Scripture quotations taken from the Holy Bible, New International Version®, NIV®. Copyright © 1973, 1978, 1984, 2011 by Biblica, Inc.™ Used by permission of Zondervan. All rights reserved worldwide. www.zondervan.com.

Any *italic* in Scripture quotations has been added by the author for emphasis.

Interior design by Michael J. Williams

Library of Congress Cataloging-in-Publication Data

Names: Wittmer, Michael Eugene, author.
Title: Anticipating heaven / Michael Wittmer.
Description: Grand Rapids, Michigan : Discovery House, [2019] | Series: Our Daily Bread guides to everyday faith | Includes bibliographical references and index.
Identifiers: LCCN 2018061297 | ISBN 9781627079273 (pbk. : alk. paper)
  Subjects: LCSH: Heaven--Biblical teaching. | Future life--Biblical teaching. | Death--Biblical teaching.
Classification: LCC BS680.H42 W58 2019 | DDC 236/.24--dc23
LC record available at https://lccn.loc.gov/2018061297

ISBN: 978-1-62707-927-3
Printed in the United States of America
21 22 23 24 25 26 27 28 / 10 9 8 7 6 5 4 3

CONTENTS

HOW DO I DO THIS?

My dear friend was dying from cancer. One evening her husband of more than fifty years phoned, "Can you come over? We're not sure Jan is going to make it through the night."

I hurried to their condo and found Jan lying on the couch. She wasn't in apparent pain, but her pale complexion and frail voice indicated the end might be near. She thanked me for coming and got straight to the point. "How do I do this?" she asked. "I've never died before."

I stammered for a minute, stalling for time. What a question! It's a question we all should be asking;

and we're wise to ask it early, before we're in range, before death is on the move.

I said some silly things as I fumbled for answers. But then God gave me a word for His beloved daughter: "Jan, *you* don't do this. You've walked with Jesus for more than seventy years, for this very night. Tonight it all pays off. This is the night you cash in. *How do you do this?* You don't. You don't do anything tonight but climb on Jesus's back and let Him carry you to the other side. You let Him do all the heavy lifting. You don't do anything tonight but go to sleep in Him."

Jan did not die that night. She survived several more months, but she was ready to go because she knew what was coming. She loved the Scriptures, and her final days were filled with biblical dreams of heaven, Jesus, and loved ones who had gone before. She could die well because she trusted her faithful Lord and Savior.

This book is about Jan's present, and also her future. *What happens when believers in Jesus die,* and *what happens after that?*

This book is about your future, and also your present.

Have you noticed that the final score gives meaning to what happens during a game? If a star player scores fifty points and his team wins by one, he will be hailed as a hero who carried his team and refused to lose. If the same player scores fifty points and his team loses by one, he may be criticized for hogging the ball and not trusting his teammates. Same player, same game, but a slightly different outcome changes how fans analyze his play.

Life is not a game, but its point does come from the final score. Our future interprets our present. What happens in our next life gives meaning to what happens in this one. To change analogies, if we want to know what life's journey means, we have to know where we're going. Our destination is the point of our trip.

What does your life mean now? It all depends on where you're going. It all depends on what happens after you die, and what happens after that.

Have you given your life to Jesus? Then turn the page. This is your future. And because it's your future, it's also the meaning of now.

CHAPTER 1

PRESENT WITH JESUS

What happens the moment we die?

The Bible doesn't supply a lot of details, but here's what we know for sure. Jesus told the believing thief on the cross, "today you will be with me in paradise" (Luke 23:43). The apostle Paul said he longed "to depart" this life "and be with Christ, which is better by far" (Philippians 1:23). Death might separate Paul from his body, but it would also take him "home" to be with the Lord (2 Corinthians 5:8). Paul believed his personal hope was true of all Christians. When Jesus returns He will bring along "those who have fallen asleep in him." He will raise their bodies from the grave and call up those still living "to meet the Lord in the air. And so we will be with the Lord forever" (1 Thessalonians 4:14–17).

These passages all say the same thing: when believers die, we are with the Lord. Some Christians believe we must endure a period of purification to prepare for the presence of God. I understand why they might think that, but neither Jesus nor Paul seemed to agree. Jesus told a sinful and dying man that they would be together *today* and Paul said he desired "to depart and be with Christ," not "depart and prepare to be with Christ." So it seems the moment we die we are with the Lord.

But are we awake? Some Christians notice that Jesus will bring "those who have fallen asleep" and wonder whether we take a long nap when we die. Scripture often does describe death as sleep—Stephen, David, and some who had seen the risen Lord "fell asleep."[1] But this seems to be a euphemism—a gentle way to describe death—that should not be taken literally. When Jesus determined to raise Lazarus from the dead, He broached the subject by telling His disciples, "'Our friend Lazarus has fallen asleep; but I am going there to wake him up.' His disciples replied, 'Lord, if he sleeps, he will get better.' Jesus had been speaking of his death, but his disciples thought he meant natural sleep. So then he told them plainly, 'Lazarus is dead'" (John 11:11–14). Let's avoid the mistake of the overly literal disciples. As subsequent chapters will discover, the saints in heaven right now are worshiping God, which means they are very much awake.

Alive

So it seems the moment we die is when we see Jesus. What a juxtaposition! Our weakest moment is immediately followed by our very best. One moment we are at the end of our rope, with no strength to go on. We are never more helpless than at the moment we die, never more dependent on others. What will happen to our body? Will it be respectfully cared for? That depends on others. We're dead, and soon our body will start to rot.

But as we leave this life in the worst possible condition, we instantly become alive in the presence of Jesus. He is our highest good, our one true love, our reason for living. The meaning of our entire existence, both before and after, is compressed into this single epic moment. This moment is what we've been aiming for. Every wholesome pleasure, every joy, every deep satisfaction has been leading us to Jesus. We are finally home, forever with our Lord.

Have you ever thought about this first time you meet Jesus? What will you say? What will you do first? Will you greet Him with a fist bump or a handshake? "Hello, my name is _____." Perhaps a hug or a high five? Nope.

Will you blurt out the burning questions that have long bothered you? *Can you please tell me why my child got cancer? Why did you allow that distracted driver to plow into my car? Why didn't you stop the Holocaust?* Perhaps your first thought will be theological: *How exactly does the Trinity work? How are you both infinite God and finite man? Was your temptation real if you couldn't sin? Who wrote Hebrews?* No, no, no.

Here's how this is going to go. When the apostle John saw a vision of his glorified Lord, with hair "as white as snow," eyes "like blazing fire," and a voice "like the sound of rushing waters," John "fell at his feet as though dead" (Revelation 1:12–17). If this happened to Jesus's closest friend, how will we—who "have not seen him" yet (1 Peter 1:8)— respond? We too will unravel in His presence. We'll fall at His feet and proclaim, "My Lord and my God!" Then Jesus will place His nail-scarred hand on our shoulder and say something like, "'Do not be afraid. I am the First and the Last. I am the Living One; I was dead, and now look, I am alive for ever and ever!' And so are you" (Revelation 1:17–18).

There will be tears, a long embrace, and special words for each of us. Jesus promises to give us each "a white stone with a new name written on it, known only to the one who receives it" (Revelation 2:17). Scholars debate the significance of the white stone—it may be an award given to victorious saints, a token for admission to the messianic banquet, what jurors would use to vote for acquittal, or simply a clean, common surface for inscriptions. Whichever it is, God promises the new name it contains will wipe away our shame (Isaiah 62:1–4). Our new, personalized name indicates both our new, redeemed identity and our unique intimacy with the Lord. Jesus will not relate to us with an off-the-rack, one-size-fits-all love. He isn't a mall Santa, greeting us each with the same assembly-line questions. Jesus will love us individually, with a name that only He and we know.

While our initial meetings will vary depending on our unique relationship, we all will be awash in gratitude. In this life, we are thankful when someone saves us from making a mistake, especially if it is potentially damaging or embarrassing. *Are you sure you want to wear that? Everyone else will be dressed up.* We are even more thankful when someone rescues us from financial ruin or a serious accident. *Here's a loan that will get you through the first of the year.* Or, *Your harness wasn't fastened securely. Now you're ready to jump.* Imagine how thankful we will be when we meet the One who saved us from hell. What words could possibly express our gratitude?

Loved

But wait, it gets better. Jesus didn't merely save us *from* something—that would be more than enough—He also saved us *for* something. Or more properly, for *Someone.* Jesus didn't merely save us from hell and for everlasting life. He saved us for himself. He promised the disciples He must leave to prepare a place for them: "and if I go and prepare a place for you, I will come back and take you to be with me that you also may be where I am" (John 14:3). This is unfathomable but true. Jesus doesn't only want to *save* you. He wants *you.* Jesus yearns for a relationship with you, and He won't be satisfied until you see Him face to face.

Our relationship cannot be restored without forgiveness, and so Jesus will forgive all of our sin. He has already paid our entire debt. We don't always believe that, but all doubt will melt away when we see Jesus. In that moment we will feel all the way to our toes that we are fully known. Jesus "will bring to light what is hidden in darkness and will expose the motives of the heart" (1 Corinthians 4:5). We cannot hide one stray thought from the piercing gaze of our holy God. This should terrify us, and it would, except that we'll also sense deep in our bones that we are fully loved. We will know that Jesus knows everything about us, and wants us anyway.

That is all we can ask for and way more than we deserve. But again, it gets better.

Fixed

In that moment when we see Jesus, we will realize we're not only forgiven; we're also fixed! In this life we often muddle through, having good days and bad, "but we know that when Christ appears, we shall be like him, for we shall see him as he is" (1 John 3:2). Jesus will perfect us in righteousness, taking away both our desire and our ability to sin and reject Him.

This will be necessary for our long-term relationship. Think of it like this: When marriage vows are broken through adultery or abuse, some relationships never recover even if the couple remains married. Although his spouse may forgive his sin, the offender realizes he is still the same person who did those things, just forgiven. He continues to be embarrassed by what he's done and for who he is. He may often blow up at his wife for being "the good one." Or sulk and berate himself for being the cause of all their problems. Their relationship is too lopsided to work. One is in the "right" and the other will always be in the "wrong."

Our relationship with Jesus will be lopsided too, but only because He is the infinite God-Man and we are His finite creatures. This inequality is fine because we are supposed to be creatures. Finitude shouldn't bother us any more than a dog is unhappy wagging her tail or hiding a bone. She's a dog, and she enjoys doggy things. We're human, and we enjoy human things. Our relationship with Jesus is lopsided because we are finite, but it will not be lopsided because we are fallen. Jesus will fix that the moment we see Him. Paul explains, "Those he predestined, he also called; those he called, he also justified; those he justified, he also glorified. . . . Who then is the one who condemns? No one." There is nothing left to spoil our relationship, nothing that can "separate us from the love of God that is in Christ Jesus our Lord" (Romans 8:30–39).

We may wince when we remember the specific sins Jesus saved us from, but we'll also know that isn't who we are anymore. We won't enter the next life humiliated because of who we are, mad at ourselves for continually messing up and mad at Jesus for always taking the high road. We'll start out glorified, cleansed from sin and confirmed in righteousness. We'll be forgiven by grace, and changed by it too.

Rewarded

But wait, it gets better. Jesus will not only forgive and fix us from all sin, He also will reward us for whatever good we have done in His name. Our works don't have to be spectacular. Jesus will reward adventurous acts of faith, such as starting a Christian ministry or preaching the gospel to stadiums of people. And He will reward the everyday acts of loving our enemies, keeping our word, putting in an honest day's work, and sharing our stuff with those in need. Jesus said "anyone who gives you a cup of water in my name . . . will certainly not lose their reward" (Mark 9:41). However many talents we have, we all may hear from our Lord, "Well done, good and faithful servant! You have been faithful with a few things; I will put you in charge of many things. Come and share your master's happiness!" (Matthew 25:23).

Your most momentous moment could come at any time. It will occur either when Jesus returns or the moment you die. In that pivotal moment you will know that you've been saved from hell and for Jesus. You've been forgiven, fixed, and you're finally home, to live forever with the divine, Middle Eastern Man who died for you. Best of all, you're just getting started.

CHAPTER 2

ENTHRALLED
IN WORSHIP

What happens when followers of Jesus die? Much of what Christians think about heaven comes from our imagination, possibly even the imaginations of filmmakers, or from reports of those who claim they died, went to heaven, and came back. While many of us are encouraged by their stories, I will focus our understanding on what we find in Scripture.

The apostle Paul apparently visited heaven but kept its secrets to himself. He said he "heard inexpressible things, things that no one is permitted to tell" (2 Corinthians 12:2–4). So we won't learn much from him. The apostle John also was caught up to heaven, and he was told to write down what he saw (Revelation 1:11). We'll rely on his experience in the book of Revelation to learn what God says happens when believers die.

As we learned in the last chapter, the one thing we know for sure is we'll be with the Lord. And if we're with the Lord, we assume we'll be worshiping, because that's what you do when you're in the presence of God. Here's why that matters, and what it may be like.

Earthly Longing

When in this life have you felt most satisfied? It depends. God made us for both activity and rest, and each brings its own kind of joy.

Because God made us for rest, it's hard to beat the quiet pleasure that washes over us after dinner in a cottage on a lake, as dusk falls and stars come out, the sound of bullfrogs and the laughter of family and friends filling the air. We smile and say to ourselves, *This! I was made for this!* We also feel deep contentment when we curl up on the couch for a Sunday afternoon nap, in that teetering moment between wakefulness and sleep, just before the shades fall across our eyes. Wow. Writing those words makes me want to lie down. And we feel profound joy when some melodious chord stirs our core, such as the trumpet tune in Copland's "Simple Gifts" or the violin riff in *Wicked*'s "Dancing through Life." We jump out of our chair to air conduct an imaginary orchestra. We have to move, because God made us for activity too.

So let's talk about action. What activity has brought you the most satisfaction? We feel deep pleasure when we finish a project and hit print, strike a ball in the sweet spot of our bat or club, hear an engine sputter to life and purr after a week's worth of wrenching, or when we come to the end of a performance we know we nailed. If we're a gymnast or ice skater, we may pump our fists, point to the sky, then bow as the crowd stands to cheer our success. Waves of applause crest over us. Does it get any better than this?

Actually, yes. Our joy in these moments is directed at ourselves. This is a start, but we need more. If we are the end of our joy, then our joy ends with us. We may be perfectly happy with ourselves and what we've accomplished, but then what? We intuitively know we've got to include others, and so athletes who just won a championship hoist the trophy over their head and say, "This is for you, Cleeeeeveland!" (My Cleveland teams almost never win, so I've heard this phrase exactly once, which is why it stuck.) The championship means more when we convince ourselves we won it for someone else. Our joy multiplies when we aim it at others, who echo back our joy and pass it on to their friends. *Did you see the game? What a play!*

Glory shines brighter the more it is shared. This is evident in our glorious, triune God—three divine Persons who happily praise and serve each other. Their praise itself is an important form of their service. The Father serves the Son when He says, "This is my Son, whom I love; with him I am well pleased" (Matthew 3:17). The Son serves the Father when he says, "the Father is greater than I" (John 14:28). The Spirit glorifies the Son, who in turn honors the Spirit and glorifies the Father, who responds by glorifying the Son and protecting the dignity of the Spirit.[1] Read the Gospels, and you'll notice each divine Person would rather praise the Others than talk about His own accomplishments.

This triune God created us in His image, so we shouldn't be surprised that our highest satisfaction comes from praising others. Who doesn't enjoy telling a child or student they did well? Who isn't thrilled to cheer a game-winning play, write a thank-you note to a mentor, or tell an author what their book meant to you? Jimmy Fallon has a recurring bit on *The Tonight Show* where individuals tell a poster how much the actor on the poster has inspired them. When they finish, the actor steps from behind a curtain and thanks them for their kind words. Most of the individuals scream and dance with delight. As much as their words encourage the actor, it's clear the experience means more to the people expressing thanks.

Of course, our praise only counts when it's sincere. We're not really praising our kids when we give everyone on the soccer team a Most Valuable Player Award. Or when we say they're amazing for doing their chores. Or when my dental hygienist gushes over my "home care." (Yes, I brush and floss my teeth. Doesn't everybody?)

Heavenly Satisfaction

If we are most satisfied when we genuinely praise others, then our greatest possible satisfaction comes from giving our most exuberant praise to the highest Other. This is what we were made for. This is the promise of heaven. Scripture's most extensive glimpses of heaven occur in John's Revelation, which grasps for images to convey God's glorious throne room. John said he noticed "a door standing open in heaven." He was taken up and through, where he saw

> a throne in heaven with someone sitting on it. And the one who sat there had the appearance of jasper and ruby. A rainbow that shone like an emerald encircled the throne. Surrounding the throne were twenty-four other thrones, and seated on them were twenty-four elders. They were dressed in white and had crowns of gold on their heads. From the throne came flashes of lightning, rumblings and peals of thunder. In front of the throne, seven lamps were blazing. These are the seven spirits of God. Also in front of the throne there was what looked like a sea of glass, clear as crystal. (Revelation 4:1–6)

Notice how John's description is the opposite of most photographs. It's in focus on the edges and fuzzy in the center, the closer it comes to the throne. John may have been unable to fully capture what he saw, but he wasn't making it up. His vision is consistent with descriptions of heaven in Ezekiel 1, Daniel 7, and Isaiah 6. Still, Revelation is a notoriously difficult book to interpret. Here's what we can say for sure about our worship in heaven, and what we should say a bit more tentatively.

In John's vision, four cherubim and twenty-four elders praise God continuously for *who He is*—"'Holy, holy, holy is the Lord God Almighty,' who was, and is, and is to come." They also praise Him for *what He has done*. They praise God for his glorious *creation:* "You are worthy, our Lord and God, to receive glory and honor and power, for you created all things, and by your will they were created and have their being" (Revelation 4:8–11). And they praise God and the Lamb for His more glorious *redemption:* "You are worthy . . . because you were slain, and with your blood you purchased for God persons from every tribe and language and people and nation." Then many angels shout, "Worthy is the Lamb, who was slain, to receive power and wealth and wisdom and strength and honor and glory and praise!" Their cries seem to awaken the rest of the world, as John then "heard every creature in heaven and on earth and under the earth and on the sea, and all that is in them, saying: 'To him who sits on the throne and to the Lamb be praise and honor and glory and power, for ever and ever!'" (5:9–13).

If worshiping God is our highest possible activity and pleasure, may we assume worship is the only thing we will do in heaven? Maybe. John's vision of heaven in Revelation 4–5 includes cherubim and angels—"thousands upon thousands, and ten thousand times ten thousand" angels (5:11)—but no clear mention of humans. The twenty-four elders might represent the church, Old Testament saints, or all of God's people, but many commentators think they are not human at all but rather an exalted order of angels who continuously worship around the throne.

Humans do not indisputably appear in John's vision of heaven until Revelation 6 and 7. There we learn that the martyred saints of "the great tribulation," "a great multitude that no one could count," stand "before the throne of God and serve him day and night in his temple" (7:9–15). What might "serve him day and night" mean? There are several possibilities:

1. It may imply that saints in heaven do nothing but continuously praise God. In Revelation 3, Jesus did promise the Christians in Philadelphia that "the one who is victorious I will make a pillar in the temple of my God. Never again will they leave it." But this is probably a metaphorical description of the Christian's security. Ancient pillars were often inscribed. In this case Jesus promises to write on us "the name of my God and the name of the city of

my God . . . and . . . my new name" (3:12). Unlike names that can be chiseled off pillars, and unlike pillars from lesser temples that are easily toppled, we will be immovable pillars bearing permanent names in the everlasting temple of God.

2. It might be hyperbole—an exaggerated way to explain our main business of heaven. Luke wrote that the prophetess Anna "never left the temple but worshiped night and day, fasting and praying" (2:37). I doubt Luke meant this literally, that Anna did nothing but pray and fast around the clock. She must have stopped to eat and sleep sometime, or she wouldn't have made it to age eighty-four!

3. Or perhaps "day and night" doesn't mean 24/7 but merely a full day, analogous to the Jewish offering of both morning and evening sacrifices (Exodus 29:38–41).

4. Or perhaps it does mean 24/7, and intends to contrast the glory of heavenly worship with its more limited version on earth. Unlike the Jerusalem temple, which shut its gates after the evening sacrifice, those cleansed by the perfect sacrifice of Christ may stand in His presence without interruption (Ezekiel 46:1–3; Hebrews 9:11–14).

Whatever serving God "day and night in his temple" means, we can trust God to give us the perfect amount of heavenly activity and rest. God describes the goal of our salvation as "Sabbath-rest," and He urges us to "make every effort to enter that rest" (Hebrews 4:8–11). Sabbath rest on earth includes time for worship, and it also includes time for rest. We won't stop being human when we go to heaven. We'll still be creatures, which means we may need periods of rest. As this chapter noted at the top, timely rest is pleasurable in its own right.

So perhaps the saints as a whole will "serve him day and night," while individual saints may stop and start. This seemed to be God's arrangement for the musical Levites in the Old Testament temple (1 Chronicles 9:33). Or perhaps God will supernaturally sustain us so we all will worship without breaks. Either way, whether we are worshiping or resting, or whether our worship is itself rest or our rest a form of worship, we will continuously experience the deepest satisfaction that a human being can feel.

When in your life have you felt most satisfied? If you're a Christian, it may have happened during worship. You enthusiastically sang yourself hoarse to the Lord: "Love divine, all loves excelling, joy of heaven, to earth come down . . ." The melody lifted your heart to heaven, and you found yourself "lost in wonder, love, and praise." As inspiring as that moment was, it was only an appetizer for the Marriage Supper of the Lamb. The main course is still to come, and it's going to be great.

CHAPTER 3

BOUND IN HEAVENLY COMMUNITY

What happens when Christians die? The Bible doesn't supply many details, but one thing we know for sure is that we are with the Lord. And if we're with the Lord, we assume we are worshiping, because that's what you do when you're in the presence of God. What could be more satisfying than praising our triune God—the One who sits on the throne, the Lamb at the center of the throne, and the sevenfold Spirit who blazes as lamps before the throne (Revelation 4:2–5; 7:17)? Only this: to praise this highest Other in a jubilant community of redeemed others. That would be better, and it's precisely what Scripture promises.

In John's vision of heaven, he sees

a great multitude that no one could count, from every nation, tribe, people and language, standing before the throne and before the Lamb. They were wearing white robes and were holding palm branches in their hands. And they cried out in a loud voice: "Salvation belongs to our God, who sits on the throne, and to the Lamb." (Revelation 7:9–10)

Unity and Diversity

The first thing John notices is the size of this joyful assembly: "a great multitude that no one could count." This endless throng of redeemed people fulfills God's promise to Abraham, that all the people on earth would be blessed through him, and that his spiritual children would number more than the stars in the sky or the sand on the shore.[1] This promise seemed impossible when God made it, as Abraham and Sarah were old and childless; and its fulfillment was still far away when John wrote his words, as the church was still quite small at the end of the first century. It would take a miracle for the church to swell to uncountable numbers. And so it has.

The second thing John notices is the crowd's diversity. These worshipers come from "every nation, tribe, people and language." There is no more diverse group than the church. That's not only great fun—(Have you ever eaten at a multiethnic potluck or participated in a multiracial worship service?), it's essential.

Community requires both unity and diversity. I can't have community with myself; I can only have community with other people. And the more different they are from me, the more potential for profound, life-enriching friendship. If we only hang around people like ourselves, we're just a clique. Our most exciting community happens when opposites attract—men meet women, Jews mix with Gentiles, slaves mingle with masters, urban professionals socialize with rural blue-collar workers, Republicans talk to Democrats, socialists get to know capitalists, and so on.

But diversity only takes us so far. Community requires a magnetic center that pulls everyone in. What could unite people from every tribe and nation? Certainly not democracy, not the English language, not even the Olympics. The only centripetal force that can permanently bind us together is Jesus.

The people in John's vision "were wearing white robes and were holding palm branches." White symbolizes purity, as they and their robes were washed "in the blood of the Lamb" (Revelation 7:14). Palm branches signify victory—not what they won on their own but the battle that Jesus won for and with them. John lived in Ephesus, and he would have been familiar with his city's frieze of the goddess Nike who, in the shape of the trademark swoosh, triumphantly held a victor's wreath in her left hand and a palm branch in her right. When he saw the palm branches and heard their praise, "Salvation belongs to our God, who sits on the throne, and to the Lamb," John knew he was witnessing heaven's victory celebration.

Most of us have won something—a race, a raffle, a promotion, someone's heart. Do you remember how happy you were? You shared your joy with a few friends, and they were happy with you. Imagine the joy of heaven. We will not celebrate something small or with a select group. We will praise God for our great salvation, our voices merging with others as far as the eye can see.

And not just our voices but our lives. An orchestra doesn't tune section-by-section down the line, with the violins tuning the clarinets, who tune the trumpets, who tune the French horns, and so on. By the time the tuning came to the trombones, the pitch would have been lost. Instead, each section in the orchestra tunes with a single oboe. As each instrument falls in line with the oboe, it automatically is tuned to every other instrument. In the same way, as we tune our hearts to Jesus, our hearts are automatically tuned to every other worshiper. Our salvation is personal but it's not individual. We will never be lonely again.

Kings and Priests

Every community needs a purpose. Florida retirement communities sometimes fall apart because too many people have too much free time and they become bored and get into each other's business. Deepest community is forged when the stakes are high and we're fighting for a common goal. This is why army battalions form friends for life. No one else understands what this band of brothers endured, and the experience binds them forever.

What is the purpose of our heavenly community? Definitely to praise God for saving us. But there's something else. This may come as a surprise, but our role in God's battle isn't finished when we get to heaven. There's more to come.

We've noted John's phrase, "every nation, tribe, people and language." A similar expression appears two chapters earlier, in Revelation 5:9–10. There we learn God has purchased "persons from every tribe and language and people and nation," and He has made this redeemed community "to be a kingdom and priests to serve our God, and they will reign on the earth."

Wait. What?! God has prepared His saints in heaven to "reign on the earth?" Why would we ever want to leave heaven to do that? I'll say more about this in future chapters. For now, take this promise as a hint that going to heaven is not our final end. Our story continues, and it's tied to our identity as kings and priests. This is not the only time John calls us this. He opens Revelation by saying Jesus "has made us to be a *kingdom and priests* to serve his God and Father" (1:6), and he closes Revelation by promising we "will be *priests* of God and of Christ and will *reign* with him for a thousand years" (20:6).

To understand what it means to be God's kings and priests—and why that requires us to live on earth—we have to start in the beginning. God created humanity in His image to rule as *kings* over this world on His behalf. He said, "Let us make mankind in our image, in our likeness, so that they may rule over the fish in the sea and the birds in the sky, over the livestock and all the wild animals, and over all the creatures that move along the ground" (Genesis 1:26).

God also created us to serve as His *priests.* He "took the man and put him in the Garden of Eden to work it and take care of it" (Genesis 2:15). The Hebrew words for "work" and "take care of" (*'ābad* and *šāmar*) also mean to "serve" and "guard," and when they appear together in the Old Testament they often refer to priests who serve God in the temple and guard it from unclean things. For instance, the Levites "are to perform (*šāmar*) duties . . . by doing the work (*'ābad*) of the tabernacle. They are to take care of (*šāmar*) all the furnishings of the tent of meeting, fulfilling the obligations of the Israelites by doing the work (*'ābad*) of the tabernacle" (Numbers 3:7–8).

I don't think it's an accident that God used priestly terms to describe Adam's responsibilities in the garden, for Eden itself seems to have been God's earthly temple. Like other temples it faced east, from the top of a mountain, and was where God came to meet with mankind.[2] Every temple contains an image of its god. Who is the image of God in this temple? It's you and me! Our first parents were living images of God who also served as His priests. As such, Adam and Eve would have been expected to guard the temple-garden from evil and gradually extend its borders until the whole world was full of the glory and knowledge of God.

But they failed as priests and kings when they fell before the evil serpent. As goes the head, so goes the body, and Adam's rebellion took the entire planet down with him. Nothing in this world can be in right relationship with God when our kings and priests are in open revolt (Romans 8:18–22). But God did not give up on His plan. Rather, He chose Israel to be His special people who would show the world how wonderful it is to serve the living God. When He delivered Israel from Egypt, God gathered them at Mount Sinai and said, "Now if you obey me fully and keep my covenant, then out of all nations you will be my treasured possession. Although the whole earth is mine, you will be for me a *kingdom of priests* and a holy nation" (Exodus 19:5–6).

But as Adam failed to keep evil out of Eden, so Israel failed to keep other gods out of her worship. She fell into idolatry, and God used the wicked Babylonians—the very pagans that Israel was supposed to reach—to trash Solomon's temple and carry His people into exile.

Still God's plan could not be stopped. God sent His holy Son, Jesus, to be the last Adam and the true temple (Romans 5:12–21; John 2:19–21). As Jesus predicted, the Jews destroyed this temple as the Babylonians had ruined Solomon's, but He raised it again in three days. When He ascended to heaven, Jesus poured out His Spirit upon His gathered people, who are now "God's temple" because "God's Spirit dwells in your midst. . . . God's temple is sacred, and you together are that temple" (1 Corinthians 3:16–17).

Here's the point: Jesus fulfilled God's promise to Israel, which fulfilled God's plan for Adam and the human race. Then Jesus passed this fulfillment on to us, His church. We now "are a chosen people, a *royal priesthood*, a holy nation, God's special possession, that you may declare the praises of him who called you out of darkness into his wonderful light" (1 Peter 2:9).

The church will continue to perform her kingly and priestly duties on earth until Jesus returns and fills the world with His glory (Isaiah 11:9; Habakkuk 2:14). Then the entire earth will be God's cosmic temple, as He planned all along.[3]

Should you die before that glorious day, you will go to heaven and join the Lamb's innumerable, diverse community of kings and priests. With one voice you will praise Him for the great salvation He has already done, and for the greater salvation that is still to come.

CHAPTER 4

BOUND TO BELIEVERS ON EARTH

What happens when believers in Jesus die? We will worship our triune God in our royal and priestly assembly. We will rejoice in the glories of heaven, but we will not forget what is happening on earth. We will be with Christ, which means we are still connected to the faithful we left behind. We might be dead, but we still belong to the communion of saints.

Generations of Christians have recited the Apostles' Creed, a foundational confession dating back to the fifth century, which says "I believe in the communion of saints." Like the word *Trinity*, the phrase *communion of saints* doesn't appear in the Bible, but it's a concept that is basic to our belief. You may have sung "The Church's One Foundation," which mentions our "mystic sweet communion with those whose rest is won." Let's consider how this should encourage us who have lost loved ones, and what it will mean for us after we die and go to heaven.

The Communion of Saints

Scripture describes the communion of saints in this powerful passage:

> But you have come to Mount Zion, to the city of the living God, the heavenly Jerusalem. You have come to thousands upon thousands of angels in joyful assembly, to the church of the firstborn, whose names are written in heaven. You have come to God, the Judge of all, to the spirits of the righteous made perfect, to Jesus the mediator of a new covenant, and to the sprinkled blood that speaks a better word than the blood of Abel. (Hebrews 12:22–24)

Notice that "you" (the living saints) have come to "the heavenly Jerusalem" (where the departed saints are), where with the angels we are united in the "joyful assembly" of the church. Whether we are dead or alive, we remain part of the body of Christ, connected in Jesus, who is our head.

Jesus is the bond between us and our departed brothers and sisters. The same grace that pulls us to Jesus also draws us to each other, for as we converge on Christ we also link arms with one another. Nothing can "separate us from the love of Christ" (Romans 8:35). If you are in Christ and I am in Christ, then nothing can separate us from each other. Not even death. Our deceased friend or family member may have moved to the heavenly wing of the church, but we are still connected in Jesus.

Why might that connection be important to us? It allows us to talk to Jesus about our loved ones. Protestants are often suspicious of prayers for the dead because it sounds similar to the Roman Catholic practice of praying for souls in purgatory. I understand this reservation, but we should admit that Protestants already pray about the dead.

When we place the body of our loved one in the ground, our pastor commonly offers a committal prayer that entrusts our brother or sister to God and anticipates the day when Jesus will raise him or her. We pray for our physical reunion. If we talk to God about our loved ones at the cemetery, why can't we also talk to God about them months or years later? We aren't praying them out of purgatory; we're simply talking to Jesus about the people we love.

Scripture strongly suggests that the moment our loved one dies he is with the Lord. Since he is with Jesus, why can't we tell Jesus to pass on a message for us? My friend lost his daughter in a car accident, and he often tells Jesus to give his love to Laura. This not only seems right, it's also possible. Because of the communion of saints, my friend and his daughter are still connected. They may be in different wings of the church, but they are still joined in Jesus. How comforting is that!

The Reign of Christ

We may pray about our loved ones in heaven, and they also could talk to God about us. I used to think heaven amounted to a celestial hammock, where I went to relax and wait for the return of Christ. I now realize that saints in heaven may have a job that's directly tied to what is happening on earth.

A main point of John's Revelation is that heaven rules the earth. The times might seem bleak for Christians in first-century Rome or twenty-first-century wherever-you-are, but fear not, our risen Lord remains "the ruler of the kings of the earth" (Revelation 1:5). I doubt many presidents, representatives, CEOs, and venture capitalists think they report to King Jesus, but they do. Jesus twice rules the world, once because He created it and again because He saved it.

John's vision of heaven describes the moment our ascended Lord reclaimed the right to bring our world to its redemptive end. John "saw in the right hand of him who sat on the throne a scroll with writing on both sides and sealed with seven seals. And I saw a mighty angel proclaiming in a loud voice, 'Who is worthy to break the seals and open the scroll?'" No one could, and John "wept and wept because no one was found who was worthy to open the scroll or look inside" (5:1–4).

Although John was sure how earth's story would end—that Jesus was the ruler of the kings of the earth, and one day the world would "become the kingdom of our Lord and of his Messiah, and he will reign for ever and ever" (11:15)—its finale wasn't set in motion yet. God still needed to act on His promises. Our world would continue to blunder toward oblivion unless someone broke the seals on the scroll of destiny and brought history to its climactic goal. John wept for wrongs that might never be righted, sacrifices that might never be honored, and glory that God might never receive. John's hope seemed stuck. God had promised salvation, but how?

Then an elder told John, "Do not weep! See, the Lion of the tribe of Judah, the Root of David, has triumphed. He is able to open the scroll and its seven seals." Then John "saw a Lamb, looking as if it had been slain, standing at the center of the throne. . . . He went and took the scroll from the right hand of him who sat on the throne." Immediately the cherubim and elders fell before the Lamb and sang: "You are worthy to take the scroll and to open its seals, because you were slain, and with your blood you purchased for God persons from every tribe and language and people and nation. You have made them to be a kingdom and priests to serve our God, and they will reign on the earth" (5:5–10).

Through His victorious sacrifice, Jesus earned the right to open the scroll and lead creation to its redemptive climax. All of history has been pointing to that day when Jesus will reign on earth with those royal priests He redeemed from every tribe, language, people, and nation. But what about the saints who are no longer here on earth? What role do they play? One day they will return with Jesus to reign with Him. Until then, they may participate in Jesus's present, spiritual reign and anticipate His final, physical reign by their prayers. As the Lamb began to open the seven seals, each one unleashed more of God's judgment on the earth. When He opened the fifth seal, "those who had been slain because of the word of God and the testimony they had maintained" implored Jesus to go ahead and finish the job. "They called out in a loud voice, 'How long, Sovereign Lord, holy and true, until you judge the inhabitants of the earth and avenge our blood?' Then each of them was given a white robe, and they were told to wait a little longer" (6:9–11).

These martyred saints had no doubt that God would keep His Word; it was just a matter of time. God is certainly going to accomplish His final victory, but we must prayerfully wait for it. The saints knew they could not accomplish the final salvation they needed, so they rested in God's promises and begged Him to hurry.

God told them to "wait a little longer," but their prayers still seemed to make a difference. When the cherubim and twenty-four elders fell before the Lamb, "they were holding golden bowls full of incense, which are the prayers of God's people" (5:8). Their prayers—and ours—are the incense of heaven! When the seventh seal was opened, another angel "was given much incense to offer, with the prayers of all God's people, on the golden altar in front of the throne. The smoke of the incense, together with the prayers of God's people, went up before God." Then the angel took fire from the altar "and hurled it on the earth; and there came peals of thunder, rumblings, flashes of lightning and an earthquake" (8:3–5). The consummation of God's victory had begun.

Since the blessed dead pray for Christ's reign, many Christians through the years have believed they also pray for us and our role in the kingdom of God. The church father Origen wrote that "all those fathers who have fallen asleep before us fight on our side and aid us by their prayers."[1] Martin Luther told his friend, "I shall pray for you, I ask that you pray for me. . . . If I depart this life ahead of you—something I desire—then I must pull you after me. If you depart before me, then you shall pull me after you. For we confess *one* God and with all saints we abide in our Savior."[2]

The communion of saints means we never stop serving the kingdom of Christ and our fellow believers, even when we're no longer here. A soldier who becomes injured may have to leave the battlefield. He can no longer fight, but he can cheer on his comrades and pray for their success. We who serve Jesus should expect nothing less. Now we pray and work for Jesus. When we die, our direct work may be finished, but we can still pray. We will no longer be in the battle, but we can still influence its outcome by our prayers. Death may move us to the sideline, but it cannot take us entirely away from the field or from our friends who are still fighting. We simply join the "great cloud of witnesses" that cheer for our friends, urging them to "run with persever-ance the race marked out for us" (Hebrews 12:1).

As a believer in Jesus Christ, you are always connected to those who are connected to Jesus. Whether dead or alive, we remain united in Jesus, for we belong to the communion of saints.

CHAPTER 5

STILL HUMAN

What happens when Christians die? We meet Jesus, our loved ones who already died in Christ, and we worship our triune God in the innumerable, multiethnic company of redeemed saints. Because we belong to this communion of saints, we also may pray in heaven for what is happening on earth. John's vision of heaven included martyred saints who

> called out in a loud voice, "How long, Sovereign Lord, holy and true, until you judge the inhabitants of the earth and avenge our blood?" Then each of them was given a white

robe, and they were told to wait a little longer. (Revelation 6:10–11)

The last chapter noticed these saints were praying. This chapter pulls from this prayer two other important points.

Finite

The saints prayed "How long?" and were told to "wait a little longer." Do you know what this means? These saints still exist within time; they're temporal.

Sometimes we mistakenly say our loved ones who died have "stepped into eternity" or entered the "eternal state" when "time shall be no more." Eternity, however, is one important way God differs from us, and always will. The first rule of all Christian thought is that God is "up there" and we are "down here." He infinitely transcends us in every way. His perfect being is so high above us that Scripture often resorts to describing Him in negative terms. The Bible takes our creaturely limitations and says God is the opposite. We are finite, so God must be "not finite," or infinite. We are constantly changing. So God's nature must be unchangeable, or immutable. We are constrained by time. But

God has no limits, so He must be outside of time. He must be "not temporal," or eternal.

Only God possesses eternal life, which means both that He exists outside of time and that His existence has no beginning and no end. It's too late for us to be eternal, because we already had a beginning. Although God has always known us, we did not actually exist until the moment we were conceived. Unlike God, whose life transcends time and extends infinitely in both directions, our lives began at a definite point in time. Our lives will go on forever, but not because we are inherently indestructible. The same God who created our soul and body could snuff out both if He chose. He could—He is strong enough to do it—but we have His word that He won't. We know we will live forever not because we must but because God has promised to preserve us. So what we have is not *eternal life*—a life that transcends time and has no beginning and no end. Only God has that. What we have is *everlasting life*, a life that had a beginning, a life that will always exist within time, and a life that will never end.

You may be wondering, but doesn't John 3:16 say God sent His Son so we may have "eternal life"? Actually this is an imprecise translation of the original Greek. John wrote that Jesus died to give us *zōēn aiōnion*, which literally means "life of the ages." John simply said we have a life that continues forever, through endless ages. He wasn't suggesting we leave time and enter some eternal state. So a more precise translation of John 3:16 says God sent His Son so we might have "everlasting life."

We have everlasting rather than eternal life because we are creatures. That's why this discussion matters. When the saints in heaven said, "How long?" they indicated they were still creatures. This is important to know. We won't become little deities when we go to heaven (and despite popular opinion, neither will we become angels). We won't join the Godhead. We won't suddenly know all things or be able to exist in multiple places at the same time. We will never reach God's level, and that's good. What a relief to know there will always be Someone above our pay grade, Someone in charge of running the world! In heaven we will be glorified mortals: perfected in righteousness but still human, as God intended. We will still be finite, and unfinished.

Unfinished

The saints prayed "How long?" and were told to "wait a little longer."

Do you know what this means? These saints are impatient. Please understand, there is no suffering in heaven. We will experience the thrill of meeting Jesus, our loved ones, and joining the indescribable worship of the Lamb who gave His life for us. We will happily rest in the presence of our God. One of the elders promises: "'Never again will they hunger; never again will they thirst. The sun will not beat down on them,' nor any scorching heat. For the Lamb at the center of the throne will be their shepherd; 'he will lead them to springs of living water.' 'And God will wipe away every tear from their eyes'" (Revelation 7:16–17). There is no crying in heaven. But there is impatience.

These particular saints are calling out for vindication. "How long, Sovereign Lord, holy and true, until you judge the inhabitants of the earth and avenge our blood?" They had left this world as losers, slain by those who believed they should die. These martyrs yearn for Jesus to return and exonerate them, to show the world that, in fact, they were on the right side of history. That the arc of history is long, and it bends toward the Lord they gave their lives for. These saints are not suffering, but they impatiently long for something more. And God only partially answers their prayer. He gives each a white robe, signaling He agrees they are on the right side of history. But He won't yet make this known to the world. He robes them in the righteousness of His Son, then tells them "to wait a little longer."

These saints impatiently wait for vindication, and not only that. Everyone who goes to heaven will long for something more. Please read carefully. As previous chapters have explained from John's visions, heaven will be indescribably awesome. Nothing in our present experience can compare with praising Jesus in heaven's throne room. But going to heaven has never been the final goal of biblical faith. Scripture teaches Christians to hope for the three Rs: the *Return* of Christ, the *Resurrection* of the body, and the *Restoration* of all things. None of these will occur while we are in heaven.

Consider our bodies. Our present bodies do not go to heaven with us. Buried, cremated, or eaten by wild animals, they effectively go out of existence until Jesus returns to resurrect them. Only our souls make the trip to heaven. The Bible tells us we are with the Lord, and since our body is in the casket, we assume that the "us" that goes to heaven is our spirit or soul (these are two different words for the same thing).

Perhaps our heavenly souls will receive loaner bodies, as we now might receive a loaner car when we drop off ours at a mechanic shop. We may need these loaner bodies to wear our white robes and sing in heaven's choir, or perhaps the robes and palm branches and singing are metaphors that, while true, are not meant to be taken literally. We can't say for sure.

So we should be careful when talking about what our loved ones in heaven are doing. Disembodied souls couldn't hit baseballs, bake pies, or climb mountains. Besides, why should we think that bats, balls, ovens, and mountains exist in heaven? The only physical object that we know exists in heaven is the glorified human body of Jesus. Everything else is sheer guess.

There is a tension here that we must get right. On the one hand, we must not minimize the glories of heaven. What an unspeakable comfort to know that we and our loved ones who die in Christ are with the Lord! Praise God for the privilege of avoiding hell and living forever with Jesus! On the other hand, we must not frontload heaven with all the blessings of our promised future. If we receive every promised gift the moment we get to heaven, there would be no need for Jesus to return, raise the dead, and restore all things. A wise parent only lets her child open a small present on Christmas Eve, saving the best gifts for Christmas morning. Likewise, our heavenly Father gives us the best present we've ever gotten the moment we arrive in heaven. But He doesn't give us everything at once. He parcels out His gifts, so we have many reasons to pray for the Christmas morning of the new creation.

Theologians describe this tension as the difference between the *already* and the *not yet.* Already our loved ones are enjoying sweet fellowship with Jesus and the community of the redeemed. But they have not yet received all that Jesus has promised. It must be unbelievably wonderful to be a disembodied soul in heaven with Jesus. But it is even better to be a whole person—body and soul—living with Jesus here. This is precisely what Scripture promises. Praise God that we go to heaven, but this is merely the first leg of a journey that's round trip. We will rest and praise and pray in heaven until Jesus returns with us to resurrect our body, put us back together, and live with us on this restored earth.

If you're a believer in Jesus Christ, *what happens when you die?* You'll go to heaven. *What happens after that?* You'll come back, this time to reign with Jesus.

We may have left this life as losers, even martyrs for the gospel of Jesus Christ. But we will return as conquerors, kings and priests of our heavenly Father. The place of our humiliation will be the realm of our rule.

So you can be understandably excited for what will happen when you die, and even more excited for what happens after that! It shouldn't be long now. The Bible ends with Jesus's promise to come soon, and our response: "Amen. Come, Lord Jesus" (Revelation 22:20).

CHAPTER 6

RETURN OF CHRIST

What happens when we die? Every Christian knows we go to heaven.

What happens after that? Here's where many Christians become confused. They assume we go to heaven and live happily ever after. That all of God's promises come true at once: We immediately see Jesus, meet our departed loved ones, look down lovingly on friends and family we left behind, are judged, rewarded, and perfected in righteousness, worship in heaven's throne room, reign with Christ, join the Marriage Supper of the Lamb, receive our resurrection bodies, walk the streets of gold, eat from the Tree of Life and drink from the River of

Life, and probably travel, paint landscapes, write poetry, play games and musical instruments, and eat lots of pizza and ice cream (or discover that we really love brussels sprouts). Whatever we enjoyed here on earth we're now doing better in heaven. We get to do all of our favorite things with our favorite people, in one never-ending eternal moment.

Whether this thinking arises from the influence of popular culture, inadequate preaching on heaven, or the lingering effects of Plato's otherworldly emphasis on the church, running all of these events together makes a mess of our future and ignores our very nature as time-bound creatures. Since we remain temporal after we die, we should expect our future to be parceled out over time.

And it is. Heaven is far better than we can imagine, but it is not our final destination. The saints in heaven still wait for three big events, as implied in their prayer, "How long, Sovereign Lord, holy and true, until you judge the inhabitants of the earth and avenge our blood?" (6:10). They wait for Jesus to *restore* all things, to set the world right by holding sinners accountable and avenging their deaths. They wait for the *resurrection.* They have died, and are currently "away from the body" (2 Corinthians 5:8). Their souls yearn to be reunited with their bodies and be whole once more. Neither restoration nor resurrection can occur until Jesus comes again, so they also wait for the *return* of the King.

All three future events are forgotten when we think we simply go to heaven and live happily ever after. There is no need for Jesus to return, raise the dead, and restore all things if we already receive everything we could ever want in heaven. Heaven is better than we can imagine, but God tells the saints there "to wait a little longer" for the fulfillment of His promised future. We will examine each of these future events—return, resurrection, and restoration—to explain why our final destiny is far more fantastic than our most optimistic imaginings. If you think heaven will be great, just you wait.

His Kingdom

One key distinctive of the Christian faith is that the kingdom comes here. Other religions say the good stuff only comes when we leave this planet and go some other place. Muslims pray for paradise, Buddhists yearn for nirvana, and native Americans want to go to that Happy Hunting Ground in the Sky. Only Christians believe the fullness of our promised future happens right here, on planet earth.

When Jesus taught His disciples to pray, He started them out with "Father, hallowed be your name, *your kingdom come*" (Luke 11:2). Paul caught on and ended one of his letters with *Maranatha,* or "Come, Lord!" (1 Corinthians 16:22). The final prayer of the entire Bible, and its next to last sentence, is "Come, Lord Jesus" (Revelation 22:20). Christians don't pray to be taken out of this fallen, troubled world. We urge Jesus to come and fix it.

But what about Jesus's promise that He was going to prepare a place for us and would "come back and take you to be with me that you also may be where I am" (John 14:3)? Doesn't this sound like Jesus is going to return and carry us away? We must read this John 14 passage with Revelation 21, where John finishes his thought. There John sees heaven, the place that Jesus has gone to prepare, "coming down out of heaven from God" to earth. "And I heard a loud voice from the throne saying, 'Look! God's dwelling place is now among the people, and he will dwell with them. They will be his people, and God himself will be with them and be their God" (21:2–3). The biblical story ends with heaven—the abode of God, the place Jesus has gone to prepare—coming to earth.

This is what we should expect from the God whose name is Immanuel. We must stop reading that name backwards, as though it means "us with God" rather than "God with us." When President

George W. Bush wanted to invite pastors to the White House to discuss his faith-based initiative, his staff sent out advance letters alerting the pastors' administrative assistants to expect a phone call. Otherwise, they might have thought they were being pranked. What could be a higher privilege than being invited to the White House? Only this. What if the president came to your house, slept in your spare bedroom, ate breakfast with your family, and followed you around for the day? Although that might seem a little creepy, it would mean you matter a lot to him and to your country. How much do we matter to God? He isn't content to call us up to heaven to live with Him; He has promised to come to earth and live with us.

We shouldn't be surprised that Scripture ends with Immanuel coming here, because its entire story is focused on planet earth. The Bible opens with God creating our good world and us, image-bearing humans, to rule it on His behalf. When Adam betrayed God and delivered our world to the devil, God responded by promising to save this world from Satan's clutches. He would send His Messiah, a special Israelite king, to rule our world and restore creation to its original goodness.[1]

Jesus surprised many when he claimed to be this king.[2] He surprised His disciples when He said as king He must come twice. After His resurrection the disciples "gathered around him and asked him, 'Lord, are you at this time going to restore the kingdom to Israel?'" Jesus said that decision was up to His Father. For now, they must wait for the Spirit to come and empower them to testify about Jesus throughout the world. Then Jesus ascended to His Father. As He was going up, angels appeared and promised, "This same Jesus, who has been taken from you into heaven, will come back in the same way you have seen him go into heaven" (Acts 1:6–11).

Jesus came once to establish His kingdom through His authoritative teaching and miraculous signs, humble service, shameful death, and triumphant resurrection. He will come again in power and glory to consummate His kingdom by defeating His enemies and delivering "salvation to those who are waiting for him" (Hebrews 9:28). In His first coming Jesus defeated Satan by submitting to the excruciating pain of the cross (and then rising from the dead). In His second coming Jesus will defeat Satan by throwing him "into the lake of burning sulfur," where he "will be tormented day and night for ever and ever" (Revelation 20:10). In His first coming Jesus taught and modeled the sacrificial service required in His kingdom. He and

His followers win by losing, for "the last will be first, and the first will be last" (Matthew 20:16). In His second coming Jesus and His disciples will win by winning, as the last will finally become first.

Jesus will not return as the meek and lowly Savior, schlepping on a borrowed donkey from the Mount of Olives into Jerusalem. He will return as "King of kings and Lord of lords," riding a white stallion and leading the armies of heaven (Revelation 19:11–16). His enemies "will mourn when they see the Son of Man coming on the clouds of heaven, with power and great glory" (Matthew 24:30). They will hide in caves and beg the mountains to fall on them in order to "hide us from the face of him who sits on the throne and from the wrath of the Lamb! For the great day of their wrath has come, and who can withstand it?" (Revelation 6:15–17). Jesus will dismount on the Mount of Olives, splitting it in half. His army will make short work of His cowering enemies, and "the LORD will be king over the whole earth" (Zechariah 14:3–9).

Our Hope

What does the return of Christ mean for us? If we have died and gone to heaven, then we will return with Jesus's victorious army to receive our resurrection bodies and reign with Him on this restored earth. Paul promises that "God will bring with Jesus those who have fallen asleep in him." If we are still alive when Jesus triumphantly returns, then we will rise "to meet the Lord in the air" (1 Thessalonians 4:14–17). As a city sends a delegation out to the airport to welcome visiting dignitaries and accompany them back to town, so we will go up to greet the Lord when He comes to consummate His kingdom.

Paul calls this moment our "blessed hope—the appearing of the glory of our great God and Savior, Jesus Christ," and he tells us to wait for it (Titus 2:13). Jesus said we wait for His return by continually watching for it. We must not be like the foolish virgins who were caught unprepared when the bridegroom at long last appeared (Matthew 25:1–13). It has been roughly two thousand years since the angels promised Jesus would return. It's been so long that sometimes it's hard to believe He actually will. Peter warned that in the last days scoffers will say, "Where is this 'coming' he promised? Ever since our ancestors died, everything goes on as it has since the beginning of creation" (2 Peter 3:3–4).

If we're not careful, we also can start to scoff. What is your first reaction when someone predicts the date of Christ's return? I tend to laugh and say they're nuts. And they usually are. But do I think they're crazy for predicting the date—which Jesus said no one but the Father knows (Mark 13:32)— or does part of me think they're crazy for believing Jesus will return? When a news anchor rolled her eyes at another failed prediction, I felt myself smirking along with her. I sneered at the geezer who guessed wrong again. Then the Spirit smacked me across the heart. My initial response should not be scoffing but sadness that another day has passed without the return of my King. At least the old guy expected Jesus to come back! I should be so watchful for Jesus's return that every sunrise is a surprise. *It's Thursday already? I was hoping Jesus would have returned by now. Oh well, maybe today!*

We long for the return of Christ because, unless we die, that is the first time we'll see Jesus. Paul said the meaning of our lives is "now hidden with Christ in God. When Christ, who is your life, appears, then you also will appear with him in glory" (Colossians 3:3–4). We long for the return of Christ because, unless we die, that is the next time we'll see our loved ones who died in Him. Have you found this to be true? The more people we lose, the more eagerly we pray "Your kingdom come."

Christians who long for the return of Christ don't need a bucket list—things we want to do before we die or "kick the bucket." When we're in Christ, it's just not true that we "only go around once," and we'd better pack in all the experiences we can. I'm planning on returning to this world, so it's okay if I don't get to every exotic location or try every adventure in this life. I'll have forever to do what I didn't get to this time around. And because I'm reasonably smart, I'm saving bungee jumping for the next life, when presumably, if the cord is too long, my indestructible, resurrection body will only bounce. All the thrill, none of the danger!

Our blessed hope for Christ's return should change the way we pray. When I visited my friend Jan in hospice, she was slipping in and out of sleep as she dreamed about heaven. How comforting to know that was where she was going! But as I prayed with her, I didn't ask for Jesus to take her. I asked Jesus to come. To stop Jan's pain not by her death but by His return. Either way would be okay, but only Jesus's return would bring the final and ultimate healing.

Jesus did not come that day, and soon Jan passed away and her soul went to be with her Lord. Right now she is participating in the glorious worship of heaven and fighting with us by her prayers. Knowing Jan, she probably is also a bit impatient. She longs for her resurrection body and return to her earthly home to reign with Christ. She prays, "How long, Sovereign Lord?" and is told to "wait a little longer."

Jan might be early but she's not wrong. The best is yet to come. Just you wait.

CHAPTER 7

RESURRECTION OF THE BODY

Of all the featured attractions of our promised future, the resurrection may be the most controversial. A Scripps Howard and Ohio University survey found that barely half of "born-again" Christians and less than half of Protestants believe their bodies will rise again.[1] This is astounding, given that the resurrection lies at the center of the Christian faith. The Apostles' Creed declares, "I believe . . . in the resurrection of the body, and the life everlasting." Christianity without the resurrection makes no more sense than Buddhism without nirvana, Islam without Mohammed, or Hinduism without multiple gods. This chapter considers why Christians too often dismiss the resurrection, what our resurrection means, and why it matters.

A Physical Reality

We live in a secular age, when professing Christians may struggle to believe in their future resurrection because they find it hard to believe in miracles of any sort. Of course, few among us are entirely free from doubt, but if we profess to believe in God, then we must admit that miracles are not only possible, but the very kind of thing we should expect. Our resurrection is certainly incredible, but rather than cite this as a reason *not* to believe, we should take this as proof that our resurrection requires God. If we believe He exists, problem solved.

We also live in a spiritual age, when many Christians apparently reject the resurrection for more pious reasons. They focus so intensely on the "higher" destination of heaven that they lose sight of the biblical hope for the earthly return of Christ. *Why would we want to leave heaven to come back here?* They may focus so intensely on our "higher" souls that they forget the biblical hope for the resurrection of our bodies. *Why would matter even matter?*

The Corinthians were the most spiritual church in the whole Bible. They were so heavenly minded they apparently aimed to speak in the tongues of angels, and they despised Paul's simple speech. They were so spiritual they looked down on sex. They encouraged each other not to marry; if they were married, to get divorced; and if that wasn't possible, at least not to sleep with their spouse. And they were so spiritual they rejected the resurrection—both theirs and Christ's. Overall, they believed the spirit was good and the body was bad. They just couldn't fathom how raising a body would be good.[2]

Paul realized the gospel was at stake, and he devoted an entire chapter—58 verses!—to explain why Jesus's and our resurrection mattered. Here's the crux of his argument. You can tell he's animated because he shouts the same thing twice, in slightly different words. He begins by waving his hands:

> But if it is preached that Christ has been raised from the dead, how can some of you say that there is no resurrection of the dead? If there is no resurrection of the dead, then not even Christ has been raised. And if Christ has not been raised, our preaching is useless and so is your faith. (1 Corinthians 15:12–14)

He takes a breath and repeats himself:

> More than that, we are then found to be false witnesses about God, for we have testified about God that he raised Christ from the dead. But he did not raise him if in fact the dead are not raised. For if the dead are not raised, then Christ has not been raised either. And if Christ has not been raised, your faith is futile; you are still in your sins. Then those also who have fallen asleep in Christ are lost. If only for this life we have hope in Christ, we are of all people most to be pitied. (vv. 15–19)

Paul essentially says, "Congratulations, Corinthians, you are now more spiritual than God. You are so heavenly minded you're not even saved. If a physical resurrection is icky, then even Jesus did not rise from the dead. And if Jesus remains dead, then He has not been released from the guilt of our sin. He is still considered guilty and so are we. This may seem hard to believe, but your piety has destroyed your Christian faith.

Many Christians continue to minimize the body and its resurrection, even at funerals. The congregation might sing "I'll Fly Away," which likens death to a bird flying from "prison bars"; and the preacher might say the body in the casket is not really Susan, just the shell her soul left behind. The preacher might compare Susan's body to a broken down little shack, saying her death was "moving day," when she finally traded her tiny house for a heavenly mansion, and we should be happy for her because she'll never have to live in this earthly house again. Or he might say Susan's body was merely a temporary residence for her soul. As astronauts wear space suits when they go to outer space, so our souls must put on earth suits for the short time we spend here. Now Susan has shed her terrestrial suit, and she is back in heaven where she belongs.

With funeral sermons like this, is it any wonder that when I asked a class what it is that gets resurrected, one student immediately exclaimed, "Your soul!" No, our souls will already be in heaven with Jesus. The resurrection specifically targets our bodies. It's physical, or it's not a resurrection.

Perhaps you wonder about 2 Corinthians 5:1–3, where Paul describes his resurrection body as "an eternal house in heaven." He longs "to be clothed" with this "heavenly dwelling, because when we are clothed, we will not be found naked." Paul seems to be emphasizing not the location of our resurrection bodies but their source, superior quality, and present invisibility. In 1 Corinthians 15:35–49, Paul says that as our mortal bodies came from Adam, so our resurrection bodies are given by the Second Adam, Jesus Christ, who came from heaven. These "spiritual" and "imperishable" bodies will be significantly better than our present "natural" and "perishable" bodies. And unlike the Corinthians, who gloried in their visible demonstrations of power, Paul says his resurrection body is no less real for being hidden. Rather than assume Paul's physical weakness proves he is on the losing side, the Corinthians should remember that God has reserved a heavenly dwelling for him. Finally, as our heavenly city ultimately descends to earth (Revelation 21:1–4), so our "eternal house in heaven" is meant to be enjoyed on earth.

Here's another tension we must get right. The spiritual does matter more than the physical. As Jesus said, "What good will it be for someone to gain the whole world, yet forfeit their soul?" (Matthew 16:26). Yet the physical is foundational for the spiritual. Our salvation depends on the physical incarnation of Jesus—"the Word became flesh" (John 1:14)—who physically died and physically rose again. He physically ascended to the Father's right hand, and will physically return to physically raise us from the dead and restore this physical world to its original goodness. The entire story of

Scripture, from start to finish, is physical. It's more than that, of course, but it's never less. As Paul told the Corinthians, without a good physical world the gospel doesn't get off the ground.

The Best You

Perhaps you struggle with your resurrection not because you're secular or super spiritual but because you're dissatisfied with your current body. You avoid mirrors and photographs because you don't want to be reminded of the many things you dislike about the way you look. Perhaps you were born with some physical limitation, or your body has been victimized by an accident or disease. Why should you long for this body to rise again?

Here's the good news. Paul said Jesus will powerfully "transform our lowly bodies so that they will be like his glorious body" (Philippians 3:21). Our currently "natural," "earthly," and "flesh and blood" bodies "cannot inherit the kingdom of God," but must be transformed into "spiritual," "heavenly," and "imperishable" bodies. And they "will all be changed—in a flash, in the twinkling of an eye, at the last trumpet. For the trumpet will sound, the dead will be raised imperishable, and we will be changed. For the perishable must clothe itself with

79

the imperishable, and the mortal with immortality" (1 Corinthians 15:42–54).

These spiritual bodies must remain physical, for they are patterned after Jesus's resurrection body, which remained physical. When our resurrected Lord appeared suddenly to His disciples, they were startled and assumed He was a ghost. No, it was really Him and He could prove it. "Look at my hands and my feet. It is I myself! Touch me and see; a ghost does not have flesh and bones, as you see I have." They still couldn't believe so Jesus asked for something to eat. "They gave him a piece of broiled fish, and he took it and ate it in their presence" (Luke 24:36–43). What a pathetic scene! Our Lord began the day by triumphing over death, and now He closed history's greatest day by demonstrating He had the life skills of a toddler. *Look guys, I'm chewing! See, now I'm swallowing!* I'm grateful Jesus humbly proved His resurrection body remained fully physical. If Jesus will transform our resurrection bodies to match His and if He is the "firstfruits" of our resurrection—the pattern for what ours will be like—then we may assume our future bodies also will remain physical (1 Corinthians 15:20–23).

But our spiritual bodies will also be more than physical. This doesn't necessarily mean we'll be able to walk through walls or suddenly appear in rooms as Jesus did. Jesus possesses such powers because He is God, and He had them long before He rose from the dead. When His Nazareth townsfolk tried to throw Him off a cliff, He simply vanished from their sight (Luke 4:30). When His disciples' boat stalled at sea, Jesus walked out to them on the water (Matthew 14:24–25). Jesus's human body can do unique things because it is joined to deity. Our human bodies will never be united to God, but they will be vastly improved from what we are now and from what Adam and Eve were in Eden.

Our present bodies are natural, flesh-and-blood forms that we received from Adam. Adam and Eve were created good but they would die if they disobeyed God. They fell, and now each of us will die, unless Jesus returns first. When He returns Jesus will finally give us spiritual bodies that will *never die*. They will be imperishable, unable to be hurt or destroyed. Our resurrection bodies will be supernatural, spiritual physiques that are powered by the "life-giving spirit" of "the last Adam" (1 Corinthians 15:45). We will be like Jesus, fully physical and yet immortal.

And we will be fixed. If you're willing, humor me for a minute and grab your arm. Give it a good squeeze. Your resurrection body must be recognizably the one you're touching, otherwise a significant part of you has not been saved. If your resurrection body is too different from this one then you have not been redeemed, you've been replaced. This is not the Christian hope. Okay, you can let go. As redemption restores creation, so your resurrection body will fix the flaws in your current body. Scars, handicaps, disease, and obesity will be forever vanquished. There will be nothing not to like about your new body. Your body will still be you, and your best version.

This is why the resurrection matters. Redemption restores creation. Every last part of it. And so redemption must restore every last part of us. You and I weren't supposed to know we have a body and soul that can be separated. God created us as integrated wholes, body and soul, that are meant to indivisibly work together. Even now scientists can't determine where our physical brain stops and our soul begins. Our brains influence our spirits and our spirits influence our mental activity in ways we cannot fathom. As it should be.

The only reason we know our souls can be separated from our bodies is because we die. And the only reason we die is because of sin. If Adam hadn't sinned, we wouldn't die. But he did and so we do. When we die our bodies remain here, but some aspect of us goes to be with Jesus. This must be our soul or spirit, the immaterial part that survives our physical death. But our souls are not meant to be alone, without bodies, and so Scripture promises that Jesus will return to resurrect our bodies and put us back together again.

And so we wait. Especially those who are burdened with broken bodies. Joni Eareckson Tada was paralyzed in a diving accident when she was eighteen years old. She has lived more than fifty years in a wheelchair, inspiring thousands with her books, speaking, and disability center, and longing for her resurrection body that will once again leap and run and swim on God's good earth. Joni will not receive her resurrection body the moment she dies. She will receive something better, as she will meet her Savior face-to-face. She will rejoice in Jesus's presence, free from the physical pain and limitations that now afflict her daily tasks. Joni will not suffer in heaven.

But she may become impatient. With the other saints she may ask, "How long, Sovereign Lord?" *How long until you return and resurrect my glorious, spiritual body? How long until I dance with joy before you?* And with the others, she will be told to "wait a little longer" (Revelation 6:11).

Praise God that Joni's soul will go to heaven. Praise God even more that someday after that, when Jesus returns, Joni will receive her new, glorified legs and will run free on God's restored earth. And so will you. Whatever infirmities or frailties are part of your reality now, you will run free on God's restored earth. Come quickly, Lord Jesus.

CHAPTER 8

RESTORATION OF ALL THINGS

The first Christians yearned for Jesus to return in power and glory, resurrect the bodies of their loved ones who had died, and restore all creation to its original goodness. Not just the highest parts of creation, such as humans or souls, but the whole world. Peter said Jesus must remain in heaven "until the time comes for God to *restore everything*, as he promised long ago through his holy prophets" (Acts 3:21). Paul wrote of Jesus that "God was pleased to have all his fullness dwell in him, and through him to *reconcile to himself all things,* whether things on earth or things in heaven" (Colossians 1:19–20).

God intends "to bring unity to *all things* in heaven and on earth under Christ" (Ephesians 1:10).

Did you catch that? God will not rest until He has redeemed *all things*. God created a stunningly beautiful world, and He wants it all back. Theologian Al Wolters explains, "God does not make junk, and he does not junk what he has made."[1] *God does not make junk*—creation is very good. *And God does not junk what He has made*—Satan and evil win nothing in the end. Everything that sin has broken, grace must restore, and in the same order.

The Whole Wide World

The devastation of sin started with humans, but it didn't end there. As an erupting volcano blankets its locale with lava and ash, so Adam's fiery rebellion ravaged everything in its path. God had told Adam not to eat from the Tree of the Knowledge of Good and Evil, but he and Eve decided they didn't care. We can imagine what they were thinking: What if the serpent was right, and eating from the tree would make them wise like God? Maybe it was worth the risk. No one should block their progress, not even God. They would do whatever they wanted, just because they wanted it.

Isn't this what all sin comes down to? We know what God says, but often we just don't care. We want to play God, to run our own lives, to do what we want just because we want it. Our rebellion against the One Who Is Life must bring death, and the moment Adam and Eve ate the forbidden fruit they died spiritually and began to die physically. They were banished from Eden and its Tree of Life, condemned to scratch out an existence by "the sweat of your brow . . . until you return to the ground . . . for dust you are and to dust you will return" (Genesis 3:19).

Adam and Eve's sin didn't only ruin them. In horror they learned their selfishness had infected the heart of their future children. One son became jealous of another and slew his brother. How did eating forbidden fruit degenerate into murder, and in a single generation? Because deep down both sins shared the same root. When we choose to play God, we will do whatever it takes to stay on top. Cain was threatened by Abel's success and decided Abel would have to go.

Adam's volcanic eruption wrecked himself and human society and spewed through the rest of creation. Animals who were given "every green plant for food" (Genesis 1:30) now turned on each other for dominance and survival. Even the ground, from which God had formed Adam, was cursed for Adam's sin. The earth would now "produce thorns and thistles" to harass Adam and choke his food supply (Genesis 3:17–18). In sum, "the whole creation has been groaning" (Romans 8:22) beneath the weight of our sin. Adam and Eve bore God's image to rule this world on His behalf. When they treacherously turned against God, they took the entire world down with them.

You and I live on the other side of this apocalypse. Hollywood seems obsessed with apocalyptic themes, and its movies often are set in futuristic hellscapes, such as *The Matrix*, *Mad Max*, and *Frozen* (I haven't seen this, but the title sounds scary!). The truth is a cataclysmic catastrophe has occurred. This world is not the way it's supposed to be. It's not the way it was when it came from God's hand, and it's not the way it will be when Jesus is done fixing it. He's already started.

The destruction of our world began with us, and so salvation starts there too. Jesus died and rose again primarily to save people. "The Son of Man came to seek and to save the lost" (Luke 19:10). But not only people. Our salvation is the front edge of the redemption that is sweeping the globe. In 2 Corinthians 5:17, Paul writes a richly ambiguous phrase that can, and probably should, be taken in two ways: "Therefore, if anyone is in Christ, *that person is a new creation.*" This sentence can also read, "if anyone is in Christ, *the new creation has come.*" Both personally and cosmically, "The old has gone, the new is here!" When the Spirit raises a dead sinner to new life in Christ, He unleashes in that person the power that is restoring all things.

We bear witness to this cosmic power when we gather in redeemed communities, raise our children to fear the Lord, and perform every task "in the name of the Lord Jesus, giving thanks to God the Father through him" (Colossians 3:17). Our churches, families, and workplaces should be outposts of shalom—previews of coming attractions—in this present evil age. When people look at our churches, homes, and job sites they should say, "When Jesus returns the whole world will look something like that." We can't control how others see us, but we intend to "live such good lives" among unbelievers that even if they accuse us of wrongdoing, they will see our good deeds and ultimately glorify God (1 Peter 2:12).

On that day Jesus will return to finally restore all things. Isaiah says when people see Him they "will throw away . . . their idols of silver and idols of gold. . . . They will flee to caverns in the rocks and to the overhanging crags from the fearful presence of the LORD and the splendor of his majesty, when he rises to shake the earth" (2:20–21). According to Hebrews, Jesus will shake the earth to remove "what can be shaken" and deliver to us "a kingdom that cannot be shaken" (12:26–28). He will judge idolaters for their rebellion and reward us who have faithfully served Him. We will live forever with Jesus on this redeemed earth, which will be fully restored from the ravages of sin. The groaning of creation will cease, and even the animals will live in peace. "The wolf will live with the lamb, the leopard will lie down with the goat, the calf and the lion and the yearling together; and a little child will lead them" (Isaiah 11:6). Jesus died first and foremost to save sinners, yet His suffering and triumphant return also brings shalom to the rest of creation.

A Rule of Thumb

Scripture promises that after our stopover in heaven we will return with Jesus to this redeemed creation. Isaiah records God saying, "See, I will create new heavens and a new earth" (65:17). Peter writes that "in keeping with his promise we are looking forward to a new heaven and a new earth, where righteousness dwells" (2 Peter 3:13). And John closes the Bible by describing "a new heaven and a new earth" (Revelation 21:1). "In the beginning God created the heavens and the earth" (Genesis 1:1), and in the end He recreates new heavens and a new earth. First creation, then new creation.

This raises interesting questions. *What will life be like on the new earth? How will the new creation be "new" or different, and how will it stay the same?* God hasn't told us a lot, but He has dropped some clues. Second Peter 3:13 says what's new about the new earth is that it's the home of righteousness. Unlike this age, which staggers beneath the burden of sin, the new earth will be "where righteousness dwells." Notice that righteousness describes actions rather than things. Peter does not see new things on the new earth; the only difference noted between this earth and the next is how well everything gets along. God seems to agree. At the consummation of all things, the One "who was seated on the throne said, 'I am making everything new!'" (Revelation 21:5). God does not say, "I am making new things!" Instead He is taking the things that are already here and renewing them.

But isn't our present earth going to be annihilated? Peter does say God will send fire to destroy the world, as He once sent a flood to destroy the world (2 Peter 3:6, 10). But Noah's flood did not annihilate the world; it cleansed the world by washing most of the sin and sinners away. Peter seems to have in mind a smelting furnace that burns off the impurities so the pure gold remains. He uses this analogy elsewhere, writing that God sends trials to test our faith, "of greater worth than gold, which perishes even though refined by fire" (1 Peter 1:7). I prefer to think the coming fire purges rather than annihilates the world, but it's a moot point. The same God who created the earth from nothing can certainly recreate the same world if necessary. He will already do this for many people who have died and decomposed entirely. He could easily do the same for the entire world.

Regardless how we get from this world to the next, either through the earth's cleansing or re-creation, we arrive at the same place. The new earth seems to be this one, just fixed. This fits how we often use the word "new." We say we're a new person when a lingering illness suddenly breaks or when a large debt is finally paid. We aren't new in our being. We're still the same person who enjoys Indian cuisine, wiffle ball, and Barry Manilow. (Whoops! Have I shared too much?) The point is we're still us, now better.

Likewise, the earth won't be new because it's brand new but because its long struggle with sin is done. Of course, it's possible that God will surprise us and make some changes to earthly things. Perhaps grass will be translucent, animals will talk, and the West Michigan shore will be no more. Maybe, but I wouldn't bet on it. Remember, if the new earth is too different from this one, then this earth has not been redeemed but replaced. The new earth must be recognizably this earth or God didn't redeem it. And that would be a concession to Satan. If God doesn't fix this world, He would be tacitly admitting that sin has so messed up His good creation that even He can't get it back. I don't see that happening.

If redemption restores creation, here's a rule of thumb for guessing how life will be when Jesus returns and redeems all things. If something belongs to creation, expect it to be here, because that is what Jesus came to fix. If something belongs to the fall, expect it to be gone, because that is how Jesus fixes what's here. Scars, handicaps, and anything that causes sorrow should be forever eliminated. God promises to wipe every tear from our eyes, and "There will be no more death or mourning or crying or pain, for the old order of things has passed away" (Revelation 21:4)! On the other hand, I wouldn't be surprised to find lakes, mountains, and other ordinary features on the new earth. Isaiah says inhabitants of the new earth "will build houses and dwell in them; they will plant vineyards and eat their fruit" (65:21). John says the gates of the New

Jerusalem will never be shut, which may indicate trade and commerce going in and out of the city (Revelation 21:25). The new earth seems to be full of ordinary things that interact in extraordinarily righteous ways.

This may disappoint you. Perhaps you were hoping for more. Remember that Jesus will live forever with us on this restored earth. He is the *more* you've always wanted, and He will be here. Jesus will be the center of the new earth, and what a center it will be! He will sit on a throne in the middle of the gleaming New Jerusalem, which will be 1,400 miles long by 1,400 miles wide by 1,400 miles high (Revelation 21:16). Imagine a city of transparent gold that covers all of Israel, Egypt, Syria, Iraq, Turkey, and extends far into Greece, Saudi Arabia, Libya, and the Sudan. Now imagine this city is also more than 250 times taller than Mount Everest! The New Jerusalem seems to be the capitol of the new earth, the Holy of Holies in God's cosmic temple, whose glow will be visible from anywhere.

Jesus will be the center of the new earth, but there will also be a circumference. We will rejoice to worship Jesus, and we will also participate in other human activities. Adam and Eve walked with God, and they also planted flowers and played with animals. Similarly, we will praise Jesus in the New

Jerusalem, and we also will sail across crystal blue water, ride lions bareback, invent games and play them, and eat tangy fruit from the tree of life.

The new earth may seem appealing, except for you who were hoping never to come back. Maybe you've had a hard life, and you'd prefer to close the book on this world and move on. I understand where you're coming from, but think with me. Everything you don't like about your life can be traced directly to sin and the fall. When the curse is reversed, you will flat out love it here. You will reign with Jesus, in your resurrection body, surrounded by loved ones in the Lord. For the first time you will be fully human and fully alive. Jesus said the meek "will inherit the earth" (Matthew 5:5). That's not a metaphor. It's a promise.

CHAPTER 9

FOREVER HOME

The most comforting word in every language is its word for home. Everyone understands "There's no place like home"; even the crustiest curmudgeon blinks back tears when he hears the holiday promise, "I'll be home for Christmas, if only in my dreams." We all want to go home, but what exactly do we mean? We're fully home when we are with the *people* we love in the *place* we belong.

Have you asked a college student if they are going home for Christmas? If their parents have moved during the semester, they may scrunch their face and say it's complicated. They are going home, because they'll be with family. But they aren't entirely going home, because this house or this city is not where they grew up. They don't know the place.

It'll be something like this when we die. We will go home, because we're going to be with Jesus, the Person our hearts long for. But we'll be somewhere we've never been—heaven. We won't settle down there because we're not supposed to. We'll be home with Jesus, but we won't be home in every way until Jesus brings us back to live here. To correct my favorite bluegrass song, "Heaven's not my home, I'll just be passin' through." Jesus is our spiritual home and the earth is our geographical home. Jesus is *whom* we are to live with and this restored earth is *where* we are to live forever with Him.

When it comes to home, people obviously matter much more than place. We can make a new home most anywhere as long as we have our family. And if we don't have our family, no place will feel like home. Have you visited your childhood home, long after your family moved out? Memories wash over you, but you realize your former home is now just a house. The people you love are no longer there, and it is time to move on.

People matter more than place, but place still matters. Our heavenly Father is "the God of all comfort" (2 Corinthians 1:3), and He delights to give us all the comforts of Home, Sweet Home.

Our Father won't make us choose between people and place; He promises to give us both at the consummation of all things, which He describes as a wedding.

Wedded Bliss

Every wedding begins a new home. God's first word about marriage observed that "a man leaves his father and mother and is united to his wife, and they become one flesh" (Genesis 2:24). But marriage is the one good of creation that seems to disappear on the new earth. When the Sadducees asked their trick question about the woman who consecutively married eight ill-fated and slow-witted brothers (wouldn't someone have caught on after the fifth brother died?), Jesus brushed it aside by declaring "At the resurrection people will neither marry nor be given in marriage" (Matthew 22:30).

I suspect there is no marriage on the new earth in part because the fall has so scrambled marriage that God can't put one marriage back together without violating another. In a fallen world people die and divorce and the survivors of each get remarried. Many people are on their second or third spouse, through no fault of their own. How would marriage on the new earth work in their case? What if a man preferred his second wife but she preferred her first husband? You see the problem, and we're just getting started. Marriage may also go away because its exclusivity rightly lessens our openness with others. On the new earth we won't enjoy less intimacy with our current spouse (though sex seems unlikely), but we'll enjoy greater intimacy with others.

I suspect the main reason there won't be marriage on the new earth is because we'll all be married to Jesus. Paul said marriage now between a husband and wife is a metaphor that points to the "profound mystery" of Christ's union with His church (Ephesians 5:32). Marriage is not actually eliminated on the new earth. It's merely transformed into something higher and indescribable, the personal intimacy between Jesus and His churchly bride. If you enjoy life with your spouse now, consider the depth of your joy when you and he or she are united in Jesus!

Every wedding needs a place. In the Jewish world of the first century, the groom and his party would parade to the bride's home, where they would feast and celebrate for a week. So it wouldn't have surprised the first hearers of Scripture to learn that the Marriage Supper of the Lamb will occur here, in the home of the bride. John wrote, "I saw the Holy City, the new Jerusalem, coming down out of heaven from God, prepared as a bride beautifully dressed for her husband" (Revelation 21:2). As at the beginning, when a man left his father and mother to be united with his wife, so at the end. Jesus brings His heavenly home to earth.

Many Christians forget that planet earth is our geographical home, but it's obvious once you stop and think about it. We may move around from city to city, yet every home we've ever lived in has been right here. In case we still miss it, God tells us He formed the first man, *'âdâm*, from the dust of the ground, or *'âdâmâ* (Genesis 2:7). Our name literally means earthling, for heaven's sake! This means the most accurate name you can ever give your child is Clay. Or Dusty. If you have a girl, try Sandy. Or Terra. Maybe Pebbles.

Some Christians wonder if the fall hasn't ruined the earth as our home. Maybe the earth was where we belonged before the fall, but is it still our home afterward? Well, consider how you would respond if someone ransacked your home. You wouldn't say, "That's it! I no longer live here! This is not my home!" Wouldn't you say instead, "My home! What happened to my home!" Sin has ravaged the earth, but that doesn't mean it's no longer our home. It just means we care more about its devastation and pray harder for Jesus to come and fix it.[1]

Our physical home on earth reminds us not to overspiritualize the Marriage Supper of the Lamb. Our life with Jesus will be spiritually fulfilling beyond words. But our spiritual satisfactions won't exclude the physical. God delights in our physical pleasure, and He created every wholesome pleasure for our enjoyment. We should never wonder whether God wants us to have fun. Colors, flavors, music, and the smell of apple pie baking in the oven were all His idea. He created every pleasure receptor in our body, and He expects that we'll use them. God wants us to savor His physical gifts now, and He promises many more where those came from. Listen to how He describes our wedding banquet: "On this mountain the LORD Almighty will prepare a feast of rich food for all peoples, a banquet of aged wine—the best of meats and the finest of wines" (Isaiah 25:6). Jesus agrees, saying we will "feast with Abraham, Isaac and Jacob" as we "eat and drink at my table in my kingdom" (Matthew 8:11; Luke 22:30). The new earth will deliver more than physical pleasures, but it will not give less.

Better and Better

Aren't you excited to return with Jesus to this new earth? It's impossible to comprehend all that God has planned for us. But wait, it gets better! Jesus will not only redeem creation when He returns. He will also consummate it, taking it to that higher level it was always intended to go. The garden of Eden was idyllic, but the New Jerusalem will be even better. As far as I can tell, the end of our story trumps our beginning in at least five ways.

1. *Immanuel.* As explained in chapter 6, this name means "God with us." In the beginning God walked with Adam and Eve in the garden, but He came and left, came and left. The Bible's story ends with Jesus coming to live here permanently. Heaven will literally become a place on earth (Revelation 21:1–3). How good is this world? It's good enough for God. How committed is God to you? He's coming to live where you are. No longer will He come and leave; He will forever be Immanuel, indeed.

2. *Spiritual bodies.* Chapter 7 noted our resurrection bodies will be "spiritual" and "imperishable." Unlike Adam and Eve, whose bodies would die if they stopped eating from the tree of life, our perfected bodies will be animated by the Spirit of Christ himself (1 Corinthians 15:42–54). Our spiritual bodies will still be

physical, and they will be more than physical. God will guarantee that we will never suffer or die again.

3. *Higher development of culture.* Chapter 8 mentioned there will be houses, vineyards, and commerce on the new earth. The biblical story starts in a garden and ends in a city. What's the difference? Culture. God told Adam and Eve to till the garden and make something of this place (Genesis 2:15). Did they ever. Thousands of years later their descendants have produced escalating forms of culture, which seem to stay with us as we enter the new earth. And keep going from there. Imagine what heights we'll reach when the best artists, chefs, and composers have forever to create, without the handicap of sin. If you like being human and you enjoy being here, you're going to love the new earth.

4. *Glorification.* Adam and Eve were created good but with the possibility of sinning, and they did. On the new earth we will be far better off, for God will guarantee our righteousness. We will flourish in God's redeemed world, serenely resting in the peace of mind that comes from knowing God will not allow us to mess this up.

5. *Appreciation for God's grace.* There is one aspect of the consummation that is better not

despite the fall but in some ways because of it. We understand something about God that even angels don't get. Angels know God is good, but only a forgiven sinner can begin to grasp God's infinite grace. No angel has ever received God's forgiveness. The fallen angels weren't forgiven and the unfallen angels didn't need it. So they stand on tiptoe longing "to look into these things" (1 Peter 1:12).

Earlier I noted that male-female marriage is the one good of creation that won't appear on the new earth. There also are two aspects of the fall that apparently will never be fixed. Isaiah says that on the new earth, when animals again live in harmony, "the wolf and the lamb will feed together, and the lion will eat straw like the ox," yet "dust will be the serpent's food" (65:25). God cursed the snake in Eden, and He never takes it back. The other consequence of the fall that has staying power is the scars of Christ. We know the resurrected Jesus still bears His scars, because He invited Thomas to touch them and believe He was alive (John 20:27).

Consider the humble gratitude of living on the new earth. We cannot feel more satisfying, head-to-toe pleasure than we will experience there. But as we complete another morning of epic worship, lion snuggling, or delightful conversation, we'll never get full of ourselves and think somehow we deserve this. Every time we see a snake slithering in the dust, we'll remember the weight of our sin, and every time we see the scars of Jesus we'll remember the sacrifice He paid. And we'll praise Him for His amazing grace.

HEAVEN *AND* HERE

When I put my faith in Jesus as a child, I did so mostly because I was afraid of going to hell. This is actually a pretty good start. Jesus, more than anyone else in Scripture, warned urgently about hell, so He must think this is a fine reason to follow Him. I never want to minimize hell, or lose the wonder and gratitude that Jesus bore my punishment in my place.

But as I've grown in Christ I've learned to appreciate not only what He's saved me *from* but also what He's saved me *for.* In this book, I've tried my best to explain what I've learned, so that together our eyes might widen, our hearts might grow, and our tongues might tell others the good news about Jesus.

Too often we tell our friends their final choice is between heaven and hell. They may pray with us to avoid hell, but they're not too excited about heaven. *What will we do there but worship God in never-ending loops of the latest from Chris Tomlin?* That will be great for the first thousand years or so, but won't that eventually get old, even for Chris?

The first half of this book explained that while Scripture doesn't tell us a lot about heaven, what happens the moment after we die is far better than anything we've experienced yet. We will immediately meet Jesus and fall at His feet, then He'll raise us to join millions of other redeemed saints in glorious worship and prayer for the loved ones we left behind.

But this interlude between our death and resurrection—what theologians call the "intermediate state"—is not our ultimate goal. God tells us little about heaven because it's not where He wants to set our hope. He urges us to long for the three Rs: the *return* of Christ, the *resurrection* of our bodies, and the *restoration* of all things. The thrilling promise of the gospel is not only about what happens when we die, but what happens after that. We will return with Jesus to reign with Him forever in our resurrection bodies on this redeemed earth.

So the choice we all must make is not between *heaven* and *hell* but between *hell* and *here*. Hear the offer of the gospel. Do you want to escape hell and live forever here, with Jesus and all your family and friends who put their faith in Him? Would you like to praise God in His glorious presence, enjoy long walks with your closest friends, travel the world, and do whatever you wish at your optimal best? Then repent of the sin that's killing you and follow Jesus. You will become a child of God, a joint-heir with Jesus of all that your Father possesses. And what does your Father own? Look around. Someday all this can be yours. When you love Jesus more than anything else in the world, you get Jesus and you get the world too.

I love peaches, blueberries, and sweet corn. August in Michigan is the best eating month of the year. But every peach I've ever eaten has come from cursed soil. What unfiltered flavors await us on the new earth! We haven't yet seen the full brilliance of the color blue. Imagine the beauty of living with our glorious God in this redeemed world. If you enjoy being human and you enjoy living here, what are you waiting for? Give your life to Jesus, and you will inherit the earth.

These promises comfort my heart when I lose someone I love. I think often of Jan, and pray for her husband who must carry on without her. We don't know all that Jan is doing in heaven, but we know she is with Jesus, and that's enough for now. Even better, we know that any day now Jesus will return with Jan, resurrect her body, and reunite her with her family and friends who follow Him. Jan might be gone, but she's coming back. She's coming back to reign forever with her Lord who gave His life for her.

This is good news worth shouting. *What happens when we die?* We go home to be with Jesus. *What happens after that?* Something even better. It's going to be great. Just you wait.

NOTES

Chapter 1

1. See Acts 7:60; 13:36; 1 Corinthians 15:6.

Chapter 2

1. See John 15:26; 16:14; 17:1–5; Acts 5:3–6.

Chapter 3

1. See Genesis 12:3; 15:5; 32:12.
2. G. K. Beale has written extensively on the earth as God's cosmic temple, with Eden being its Holy of Holies. See *A New Testament Biblical Theology* (Grand Rapids: Baker, 2011), 614–48; *The Temple and the Church's Mission: A Biblical Theology of the Dwelling Place of God* (Downers Grove: InterVarsity Press, 2014); and G. K. Beale and Mitchell Kim, *God Dwells Among Us* (Downers Grove: InterVarsity Press, 2014). Note that although Genesis 1–2 does not explicitly say Eden was on a mountain, it must have been highly elevated since a river flowed from there (2:10).
3. Temple elements in Revelation 21–22 include: God's dwelling is here (21:3); the New Jerusalem shone with the glory of God (21:11); the city is a cube made of gold (21:16–21), like the Holy of Holies, which was a square whose walls were covered in gold (1 Kings 6:20);

the city does not have a temple because the entire city is the temple (21:22–23), the river of life flows from the throne of God and waters the garden of the trees of life (22:1–2); and only the righteous may enter the city, the wicked and unclean may not (22:14–15).

Chapter 4

1. Origen, quoted in Donald Bloesch, *The Last Things* (Downers Grove, IL: InterVarsity Press, 2004), 169–70.
2. Martin Luther, quoted in Donald Bloesch, *The Last Things* (Downers Grove, IL: InterVarsity Press, 2004), 156.

Chapter 6

1. See Psalm 72; Isaiah 60; 65:17–25.
2. See Luke 23:1–3; John 10:24–39; 19:12.

Chapter 7

1. "Poll Reveals Few Believe in Physical Resurrection," *Grand Rapids Press* (April 8, 2006), D9.
2. See 1 Corinthians 2:1–5; 13:1; 2 Corinthians 10:10; 1 Corinthians 7:1.

Chapter 8

1. Al Wolters, *Creation Regained* (Grand Rapids: Eerdmans, 1985; second edition, 2005), 49.

Chapter 9

1. Michael Wittmer, *Becoming Worldly Saints* (Grand Rapids: Zondervan, 2015), 50.

ABOUT THE AUTHOR

Mike Wittmer is professor of systematic theology at Grand Rapids Theological Seminary. He writes for *Our Daily Bread*, and his books include *Becoming Worldly Saints*, *Heaven Is a Place on Earth*, *The Last Enemy*, and *Despite Doubt*. He and his wife, Julie, usually enjoy their three teenage children. (They're good kids, really!) He punishes himself by cheering for Cleveland sports teams and rewards himself with any and all kinds of Asian cuisine. He immediately responds to notes of gratitude, and almost always to letters of concern. If you have either, you may contact him via his blog (https://mikewittmer.blog/), Twitter (@MikeWittmer), or email (michael.wittmer@cornerstone.edu). He is also on LinkedIn, but can't remember why.

Help us get the word out!

Our Daily Bread Publishing exists to feed the soul with the Word of God.

If you appreciated this book, please let others know.

- Pick up another copy to give as a gift.
- Share a link to the book or mention it on social media.
- Write a review on your blog, on a bookseller's website, or at our own site (odb.org/store).
- Recommend this book for your church, book club, or small group.

Connect with us:

- @ourdailybread
- @ourdailybread
- @ourdailybread

Our Daily Bread Publishing
PO Box 3566
Grand Rapids, Michigan 49501 USA

✉ books@odb.org